Revolving Around the Sun

A play by Dee White

Illustrated by Bruce Rankin

Contents

Pearson Australia
(a division of Pearson Australia Group Pty Ltd)
707 Collins Street, Melbourne, Victoria 3008
PO Box 23360, Melbourne, Victoria 8012
www.pearson.com.au

2019 2018 2017 2016
10 9 8 7 6 5 4 3 2 1

Text by Dee White
Illustrations by Bruce Rankin

Publisher: Sabine Bolick
Project Manager: Michelle Thomas
Lead editor: Steve Dobney
Editor: Cameron Macintosh
Proofreader: Thalia Kalkipsakis
Designer: Lisa Howard
Senior File & Asset Coordinator: Rob Curulli
Cover art: Bruce Rankin
Printed by SOS Print + Media Group

ISBN 978 1 4886 1311 1

Pearson Australia Group Pty Ltd
ABN 40 004 245 943

Characters

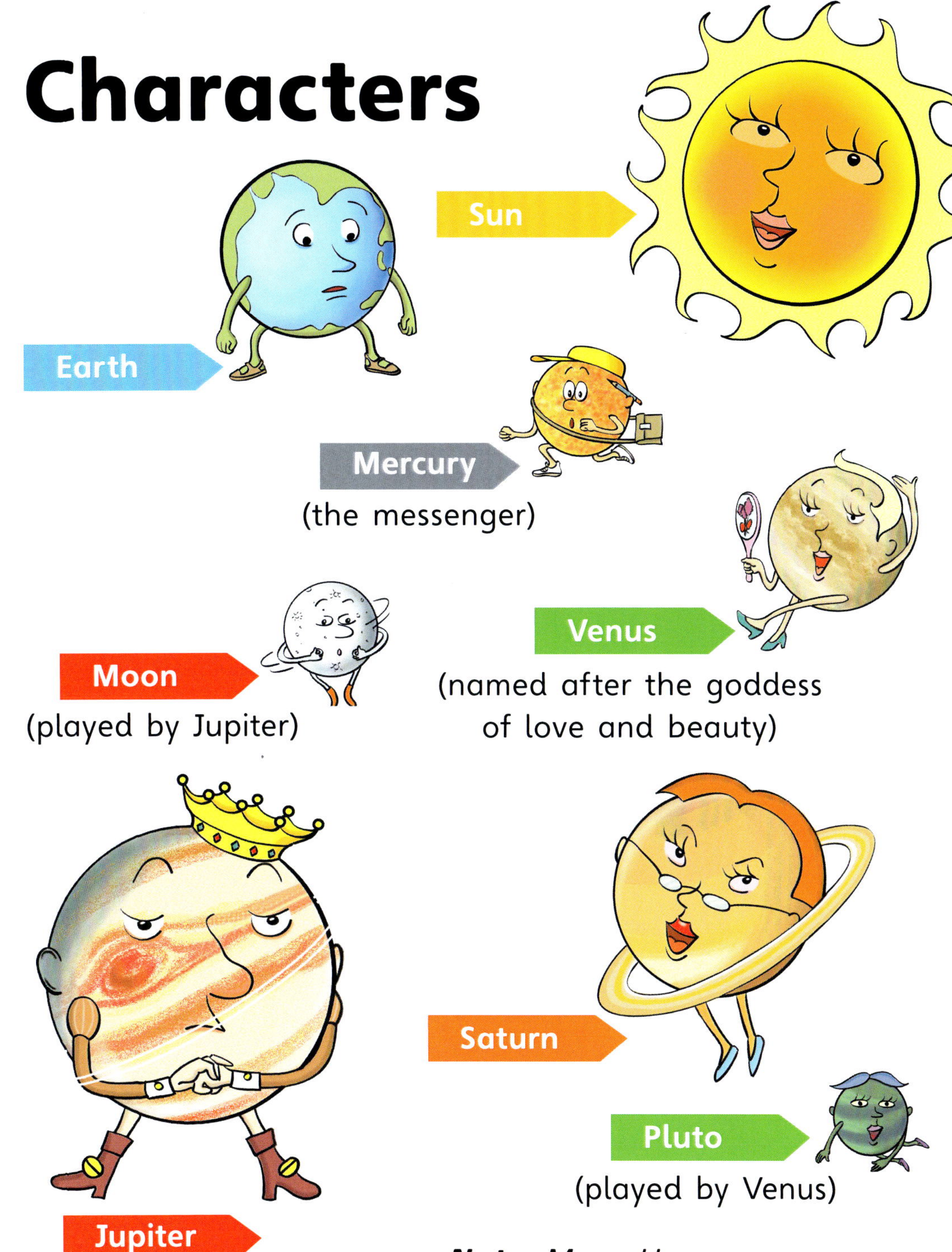

Note: *Mars, Uranus and Neptune are busy.*

Pluto
Neptune
Uranus
Saturn
Jupiter
Mars
Moon
Earth
Venus
Sun
Mercury

Act 1: The Evil Plan

Sun and the inner planets are hanging out together.

Venus: Aren't I just the hottest planet in the Solar System?

Earth: *(mocking)* Yes, and dense too!

Venus: You're just blue because I'm hotter than you.

Earth: I don't care how I look. I have more important things to worry about.

Sun: That's your fault for letting yourself go.

Mercury: Please, stop talking over each other!

Earth: Moon, stop orbiting me! You're making me dizzy.

Moon: Who's a grumpy planet this morning?

Earth: You'd be grumpy too, if you had global warming and natural disasters to worry about.

Moon: Tell a planet who cares.

Earth: Go fall in a crater!

Mercury enters.

Mercury: Stop fighting, you two. We need to talk about something important.

Earth: Shouldn't Mars be here too?

Sun: He's resting. He was feeling light-headed.

Earth: Serves him right. He's always bragging because he has less gravity than me.

Mercury: Forget Mars for the moment. We need to talk now.

Moon: What's up?

Mercury: Solar Satellite News has uncovered a plot.

Venus: A plot?

Mercury: Yeah. It involves some nasty characters.

Venus: A plot? Characters? Will there be a movie? Can I be the star?

Mercury: It's not that sort of plot.

Earth: You can't be a star, Venus. You're a planet.

Venus: Am I? Can't I be a star instead?

Sun: No, you don't burn hydrogen in your core.

Venus: (*disappointed*) Oh, I suppose not.

Earth: What's the plot?

Mercury: Some of the outer planets – Jupiter, Saturn and their little friend Pluto – are planning to steal our Sun.

Everyone stops orbiting.

Sun: They're planning to steal me? How exciting! I've been here for about five billion years. I'd love to see the view from the other side of the Solar System.

Mercury: You can't go. You're our shining light!

Sun: Thanks, that's the nicest thing anybody has ever said to me.

Venus: Don't leave us, Sun.

Sun: Couldn't I just go for a couple of weeks?

Earth: No.

Sun: (*sadly*) I've never had a holiday!

Earth: So? None of us get holidays.

Sun: But you don't want one.

Earth: Oh, yes I do! It's just that I don't complain all the time like you do. (*annoyed*) I'm too busy to listen to this.

Mercury: You'd better pay attention, Earth. You'll be in trouble if somebody steals Sun.

Earth: Why?

Mercury: Without Sun, you wouldn't have heat and light.

Venus: No heat and light? That would be awful. I wouldn't be able to see myself.

Earth: Wouldn't **that** be tragic?

Moon: You'd better listen to him, Earth. This is serious.

Earth: This is your fault, Mercury!

Mercury: Don't blame me. I'm just the messenger.

Earth: You're closest to Sun. You're the one who should do something.

Venus: This problem belongs to all of us.

Sun: I still think it's exciting. (*confused*) Who wants to steal me, again?

Mercury: I told you before – Jupiter, Saturn and their little friend, Pluto.

Sun: What do they want me for?

Mercury: They think you can help them get rich.
Jupiter thinks you're made of gold.

Earth: He's always in a spin about something.

Mercury: You know Jupiter. He's a gas planet.
He's full of hot air.

Earth: Jupiter's a legend in his own atmosphere.

Mercury: According to Solar Satellite News, Jupiter also believes that Sun should belong to him because he's the largest planet.

Venus: Isn't that bullying behaviour?

Earth: Don't worry, Sun. We won't let him take you.

Sun: (*sadly*) I really wanted a holiday.

Moon: Jupiter could be trouble, though.

Mercury: That's right. He has Saturn and even little Pluto behind him.

Venus: (*looking in the mirror*) Oh no! I think I've sprouted another volcano.

Earth: There's going to be an even bigger eruption if you don't be quiet and stop worrying about yourself!

Moon: That's funny, coming from you.

Mercury: Stop it, guys. We have to focus!

Sun: Yes, I don't want you fighting about me.

Venus: Stress gives you craters.

Mercury: (*exasperated*) I'm not sure if you all realise how serious this is. If Sun is stolen, Earth and its humans will die.

Earth: Great! That's another thing I have to worry about!

Venus: What will happen to the rest of us without Sun?

Moon: We're finished. It will be the end of the inner planets.

Sun: *(sadly)* I'd still like a holiday.

Mercury: Stop complaining, everyone. We need to think this through.

Act 2: The Atmosphere Thickens

In the outer Solar System

Saturn: Watch where you're going, Pluto! You're out of orbit, you mini mutant!

Pluto: No, I'm not. This **is** my orbit!

Saturn: You can't stay on course, and you're not even a planet.

Jupiter: *(suddenly excited)* That's it!

Saturn: What do you mean?

Jupiter: Pluto is the perfect solution!

Pluto: Thanks, Jupiter.

Saturn: What do you mean, "Pluto is the perfect solution"?

Jupiter: He has a different orbit path to the rest of us. He's the missing piece of my fantastic plan.

Saturn: What plan?

Jupiter: My plan to steal Sun! This will be the most exciting event in the Solar System for the last billion years.

Pluto: I'm happy to help.

Jupiter: Thanks for the offer, Pluto. We really need you. The rest of us are stuck in our circular orbit paths. We can't get near Sun, but you can.

Saturn: What's so good about Pluto?

Jupiter: He's special. His orbit path is oval and it's angled, so at some point he will be closer to Sun.

Pluto: Nobody has ever called me special before. This is so exciting. What do I do?

Jupiter: We'll try to push you towards Sun. Gravity should take care of the rest.

Pluto: What do I do then?

Jupiter: You grab Sun and drag her back through space.

Pluto: How far away is Sun?

Jupiter: Only about 5.9 billion kilometres from you.

Saturn: You'll be there in no time. (*aside, so Pluto can't hear*) That's if the Asteroid Belt, black holes and other planets don't get you first.

Pluto: I'll be going against gravity. How will I get back?

Jupiter: Don't worry, we'll cross that galaxy when we get to it.

Saturn: What about Earth? He won't let Pluto grab his precious Sun.

Pluto: And Mars will freeze me into an ice cloud.

Saturn: (*mumbles*) What's the problem with that?

Jupiter: You'll be fine, Pluto. Come on, let's try it!

Saturn: *(straining)* But I can't reach Pluto.

Jupiter: You should be able to get closer, Saturn. Your rings are the biggest.

Saturn: They're not arms.

Jupiter: I know. I have rings too.

Saturn: Your rings aren't as cool as mine.

Pluto: That's because yours are made of ice.

Saturn: Where are Uranus and Neptune? Why aren't they helping?

Jupiter: They don't like the atmosphere around here.

Saturn: I don't blame them.

Pluto: You'll have to stretch, guys. You're not even close to me.

Jupiter: *(puffed from stretching)* Give me a break. I've got a lot of mass to move.

Saturn: Well Jupiter, your mass isn't moving very fast. Aren't you supposed to be the almighty one?

Jupiter: (*proudly*) I am. I'm king of the planets.

Saturn: (*mumbles*) Yeah, a royal pain. You could put in more effort. You're not even trying.

Jupiter: I am trying. Look, I'm sweating and I'm a king – I shouldn't be sweating.

Saturn: This was your plan, don't forget.

Pluto: Come on, guys. We can do this. We're going for gold, remember.

Jupiter: You'll all thank me when we have Sun in our hot little hands.

Saturn and Jupiter stop trying to push Pluto.

Saturn: This is boring. You said it would be fun.

Pluto: I'm having a good time! You guys look so funny.

Saturn: Hey Pluto, why don't you go and play in that black hole over there?

Pluto: Very funny, Saturn. Jupe, you **are** sweating. You need to get fit and speed up those rotations.

Jupiter: Thanks for the lifestyle tip, Pluto. I can work out my own orbit.

Saturn: Yeah, Pluto, be quiet if you still want to be here next millennium.

Pluto: I sure do. I love hanging out with you guys.

Saturn: Then keep your comments to yourself.

Jupiter: (*yawning*) I'm exhausted.

Saturn: I'm worried this plan to steal Sun could blow up in our faces.

Jupiter: Hmmm, you could be right. Let's take a short billion-year break.

Saturn: Maybe we should give up on the idea of stealing Sun.

Jupiter: But it's such a waste of all that gold. Those inner planets aren't doing anything with it.

Saturn: What do you need gold for, anyway? Intergalactic shopping? You don't even like shopping.

Pluto: *(excited)* Can I come shopping? I could buy extra moons. I only have five.

Saturn: We're not going shopping. We don't have the gold to pay for anything ... remember?

Pluto: *(disappointed)* Oh yeah, I forgot that bit.

Jupiter: (*yawns*) Stealing Sun is harder than I thought. I'm taking a nap. I've had enough excitement for one light year.

Back in the inner Solar System

Sun: (*shakes her head sadly*) Solar Satellite News just reported that the plan to steal me has been abandoned. It looks like my holiday is cancelled.

Earth: Typical! You only ever worry about your own problems. Everything has to revolve around you, doesn't it?

Sun: Well, of course. I **am** the Sun!